Be Calm, Honey

129 Sonnets

Be Calm, Honey

129 Sonnets

David W. McFadden

Mansfield Press

Library and Archives Canada Cataloguing in Publication

McFadden, David, 1940-
    Be calm, honey / David W. McFadden.

Poems.
ISBN 978-1-894469-38-8

    I. Title.

PS8525.F32B4 2008   C811'.54   C2008-905897-6

Editor for the Press: Stuart Ross
Design: Mansfield Creative
Cover Photo: iStockphoto

The publication of *Be Calm, Honey* has been generously supported by
the Canada Council for the Arts and
the Ontario Arts Council.

Mansfield Press Inc.
25 Mansfield Avenue, Toronto, Ontario, Canada M6J 2A9
Publisher: Denis De Klerck
www.mansfieldpress.net

For Amy

     & for Ben

        & for Chloe

The three nicest people in the alphabet.

On average we're only dead for fifty-two years,
then we live again, says my friend Claude.
We'll plunge anew into the world's grey goo
from port of entry into port of call,
until we learn to see with ear and heart
that nirvana and samsara have similarities
in some way that transcends breathlessness
(it's all spelled out in the Something Sutra).

You're received by glum hobgoblins who'll review
your story from birth to death. Torture time!
But all is understood and forgiven,
just like clockwork, over in a flash.
You can be Kublai Khan someday, my dears.
No need to make a choice for fifty-two years.

Most novels in the library will feature
slippery springtimes and spectacular falls.
In some books even punctuation will sing
and sparrows will be thinking thrilling thoughts.
Moons will rise like armfuls of blue irises
while suns'll set like invisible hens on an egg.
Great auks, long thought to be extinct,
will fall in the sea. It'll seem the thing to do.

One auk smacks my window then falls in the sea.
Another falls to the deck then smacks my window.
Two of them fall to the deck then slide overboard.
Four of them smack my window five or six times.
One of them, covered in blood, drags himself
up to my window then flipflops into the sea.

3

Is it pleasant lying hidden in cool darkness
waiting for the people to dissolve?
Is it wonderful to come back out into
the warm sun and listen to the birds?
And is it difficult to find enough
insects to torment or would that be easy?
How terrific is it to be totally instinctual?
I'd love to feel that tongue licking my ear.

These lizards nesting inside the Etruscan walls
of Lombardia, it's not necessary to know
how fast they can run. One can see how fast.
Death is grim and to go slow is to die.
Homo sapiens on the other hand
are only quick at expressing opinions.

My mother loved me though I wasn't cute.
In fact I was a repulsive little brute.
Once she photographed me trying to smother
my blond-haired blue-eyed beautiful baby brother.
But *The Story of Our Baby Year by Year*
tells me that she loved and held me dear:
I was baptised in the christening dress she wore
when she was baptised twenty years before.

At birth I'm seven pounds and seven ounces.
I first hold up my head at seven weeks,
crawl like a caterpillar at eleven months,
and stand up triumphantly two weeks later.
And on my first birthday Mother was glad
to receive a moonlit rose from my dad.

I couldn't remember seeing one and this morning
I saw one in each of two separate churches:
the Virgin with a sword through her heart.
Everywhere we go we've been lighting candles
and contemplating the suffering of the saints.
We even presented both Virgins with a rose.
Both are pictured *con bambino*. Baby Jesus
has a golden saw for sawing the mountaintops.

My suffering's negligible. I never get
more than I can handle moment by moment.
Is it less than I deserve? How would I know?
Life's no big deal. As Nabokov suggests,
when things get tough just drink a glass of wine.
Hard to know how your suffering compares to mine.

What really cheers me up is when I'm having
a little chat with some old chap I know,
some undiscovered Pepys who's only interested
in the latest verses of the latest poets.
Someone who wreaks havok at a reading
while on his fourth or fifth glass of Old Sailor.
The iron door slams. It seems the two of us
will be locked in this cell for all eternity.

After the death of Christ Christians proliferated.
After World War I so did motorists.
After the Vietnam War so did poets.
Christians will sometimes slander other Christians.
Motorists seldom give each other a glance.
Poets are interested only in chance.

Lago di Como they love, they're all over it
with canoes, kayaks, sailboats, speedboats,
tourist launches, hydroplanes and yachts,
skiffs and strange one-of-a-kind inventions,
and all the latest imports from Estonia.
The Italians wear little but they love
to spend hours putting oil on each other.
The Italians of this era love their lakes.

To study the nature of vice is a virtue,
the vibrato blue of mountain, lake and sky
fully understands the underworld.
The boats go sailing slowly around in circles
and reconnoitre in the middle to meddle,
exchange news, flirt, or have a little swim.

Only you have not been lecturing me
on the virtues of the slow lane, poking along,
taking your time, counting every slowflake,
snickering when impatient people honk,
enjoying every traffic jam to the fullest,
watching the foolish present from the future,
taking your time getting out of bed,
having a catnap when the light turns red.

And then this evening on a crowded bus
everything was going far too slow,
not only the bus, but the subway and taxi,
going so slow I thought my head would explode,
as if waiting in my coffin for Judgement Day
and remembering all the things I forgot to say.

Some of us experience brushes with life —
maybe all of us at one time or another —
triggered by the intelligence of the termite
or the bashful waddle of the centipede
or those speedy cockroaches who will zip
(just because we tapped our little finger)
into a tiny hole we never noticed.
What if we happened to tap all ten?

Silly, you only tapped all ten a minute ago.
You didn't notice it but still you did.
The heart will sometimes roll out a red carpet
and little bombs will cause your brain to shrink
as if it long ago was a full-size planet
in the middle of a nuclear holocaust.

Could I borrow your ego on special occasions?
Could you let me have it when you die?
Why am I so concerned about myself?
Somewhere along the line I adopted the notion
that I shouldn't give a damn about the world.
So now when people are dying on the street
I just stroll by whistling "Blue Moon"
and thinking somebody should do something.

Compassion oozes out from every pore
causing one to think highly of oneself.
And so I stop and write a little poem
and put it in a book with all the others.
The world's in flames but lucky me I have
my exquisitely cool subterranean condo.

Golden filigree mandalas in your eyes
at Victoria Station a zillion nights ago:
neither you nor he had any choice.
You had to leave him and he'd have the same.
The portly porter suggested that you move
from window to door for a last embrace.
"You're going to have to let go of him now,"
said the skinny porter, then you disappeared.

You think of each other often and you appear
in someone's shy dream when you least expect it.
I know your reasons for silence on the subject
and I know the reasons for your solitude.
It wouldn't be right for me to speak the name
of either of you. Amazing the things I know.

Sometimes we don't know what we need until
it's on for half price at the convenience store.
How could I have forgotten I needed this,
we say, feeling half on top of the world.
We take it home, set it up, and it works!
To think that if we'd bought it when we first
remembered that we needed it, it would
have cost twice the money that we paid for it.

And it looks real nice on the front room wall.
It sounds great when I connect it to the telly.
It'll keep the dog amused for hours or more.
And tell me when it's time to sweep the floor.
Yes, I came that close to paying twice the price.
And best of all, it'll even stir the rice!

A paper without an editorial cartoon,
a cowboy reeking of too much aftershave;
ancient crypts overflowing with old car parts,
a long hot day without a gin and tonic:
I may be wrong and you are free to argue
in some boozy court in the house of verse,
but jolly women should always wear a moustache
even if it's obviously false.

I like to drink a gintónico on the porch
while a group of my favourite musicians
play sentimental love songs on the lawn.
They blush bashfully when I blow them kisses.
They love to play for me. I love to listen.
And now and then I give them little presents.

I wandered through the Veil of Forgetfulness
where scholars practise their scales all the way home,
and fulfilments arrive the moment they're desired.
Befuddled assassins done up like junior accountants
will appear on every self-help channel saying
(as they leap from the tallest tower in tinsel town),
"Once you've learned to perform a difficult skill
you can learn to do it fast and make big dough."

People who used to swear by their left wrist
no longer give themselves the time of day.
We're all online. We trust the government.
Our implants, of which we are so proud,
tell us what to do and when to do it.
Without them we'd be thinking all the time.

At first I had the Canadian radish in mind —
a ball as small as a baby's rose-red nose.
But those Shinano radishes are monsters,
and often curved like a Pleistocene tusk —
just the thing with which to point "the way"
but not "my way" as I've seen translated.
Changing "my" to "the" will dim the light
and darker jokes are fine by day or night.

Issa's poem recalls Greg Curnoe's notebooks
from his early years working for Coca-Cola
where everything was seen through rear-view mirrors.
The past tense boosts the veracity level a notch.
If Issa hadn't been so keen on radishes,
he'd merely have said, "Curnoe pointed the way."

When I heard Ernesto was being held
I hopped on a horse and rode to La Higuera,
I wanted to hear his confession, I knew he'd say,
"I'm a lost cause," and I wanted to tell him, "No,
you're no lost cause. God still believes in you."
"Father, don't rush," the campesinos told me.
"Father, they've already done him in."
Instead of slowing down I speeded up.

I'll always remember with astonishment
that I was actually there and saw it all.
He was dead and yet he wasn't dead.
His eyes were emerald and serenely focussed.
He was smiling through his own bullet holes.
In silence we waited for Che to speak.

This must have been in some other world.
The pencil I was holding and observing,
my Papermate Canadiana HB2,
was twisted like a tree in a tornado,
as if some god had turned it into putty,
twisted it to look like something scary,
then returned it to its stiff rigidity
with every twist impossible to untwist.

Another world may harbour such Mandrakes
well-skilled at performing terrible tricks.
But when I woke up was I ever surprised.
My lower right leg was severely cramped,
like a Swiss Army too long on the march,
or like a tree corkscrewed by heavy storms.

A poet's not a poet unless he thinks
he's the only poet in the world.
He knows his imperfections inside out;
he loves them as he would his fraudulent heart.
When the light goes out everything lights up
proving again darkness is an illusion.
The solar system revolves around each "I"
and every ego illuminates another.

Ninety-nine per cent of the population
has never read her work or heard her name.
Of the happy handful who happen to know her
she wishes they didn't for they've a tendency
to remind her when they invite her over for tea
that other poets are having troubles too.

Psychoanalyzing generalissimos,
fuehrers, commanders in chief, that sort of thing —
it's a tricky business best done at a distance,
hidden among the roses in the garden.
These Nietzsches see evil everywhere they look
because they never see it in themselves.
With no imagination for actual suffering
but lots of it for indiscriminate slaughter.

They must be born with an instinct for hatred.
They want to give the world a stab in the back.
They like to watch the poor cough blood and die.
But even powerless poets seem sometimes similar,
for the evil in their hearts is seldom as great
as the evil in the hearts of other poets.

Nobody could speak a word of English.
Not even the old man in the grey suit
who kept thanking me for liberating Holland
and recited Kipling's "If" in perfect Dutch.
Not even the conductor who couldn't decide
what to do with the drunk in first class
in a woman's dress and lifting it up way over
his waist to expose his dirty pants.

Not even the Italian lady who hurt herself
getting on the train and wanted me
to stroke her naked thigh and make it better.
"You are no virgin," she said tearfully,
"and you have no child, so why can't you
be nice to me and let me be your child."

Inept assassins disguised as cameramen
zoom in on Fidel in Chile in seventy-one.
They have him in their sights but neither shoots.
They put cyanide in his milkshakes
and untraceable potions that dissolve in rum.
But Fidel had sworn off dairy! and also booze!
You can get all this from Eduardo Galeano
known as he is for historical accuracy.

Bazookas, telescope rifles, a thirty-kilo
plastic bomb planted beneath the platform.
Poison cigars, but — don't forget — a Cubano
slobbers all over his stogy before ignition.
It seems God forgives Fidel for being,
as everyone knows, an "official atheist."

Yanev the cabby seems to be having an affair
with a married woman who works in the bar.
He picks her up in his cab at closing time,
takes her to his place then takes her home.
A taxi makes for an almost perfect cover.
Yanev was a professional pugilist
till he caught a puck in the eye and it left him blind.
That's not an error in the previous line.

He'd been playing a little pickup hockey
to keep his body shipshape between bouts.
Years later still the pain won't go away.
But now he and the bartender are married
and sometimes he has trouble figuring out
which kids are his and which the other guy's.

Gautama, as we know, slept on his side.
In several paintings he's portrayed that way,
plus a life-size stone-carved Buddha snoozing.
But did Christ sleep on his side or on his back?
We know Christ spent dusk to dawn in prayer
in the Garden of Gethsemane,
while waiting for the soldiers to arrest him
and whisk him off to have a chat with Pilate.

The disciples, however, lacking discipline
snored like zombies through the darkest night.
When sleepy Peter sliced off a soldier's ear,
Jesus stuck that flesh back on in a flash.
And from his conception to his crucifixion
I don't recall he ever slept a wink.

From far away, from Iran, from Japan,
they came to the monastery at Naranda.
Shantideva was known as the "eating,
sleeping and going to the toilet" monk.
He neither studied nor did he do the dishes.
All the other monks thought he was stupid.
He was an embarrassment but they
needed to get him to leave in a nice way.

So they built a special throne for him.
They invited guests to listen to him speak.
They thought he wouldn't know what to say.
But he resisted their power, and he levitated.
He floated higher and higher over the hills,
his words enlightening the monks below.

I dreamt I was a simple firefly
smiling lazily in the summer night
sending subtle messages to the others
as in the ending of *Hannah and Her Sisters*
and now when I'm sitting silently
watching my tiny wee small life fade out
I feel I'm fluttering naked in the sky
free from the agony of gravity.

When our lifelight flashes in the night
we know its span won't be very long
we live for a lovely moment then we die
but when we die we become alive
and what was once a simple blinking bug
will conceivably become a dragonfly.

Children will remind us that learning to walk
is a bigger deal than learning to play the oboe.
Over and over again we fall and get up,
each time getting closer not to fall.
Looks painful but it's fun! The distance from
the ground is slim and did you ever wonder
what baby fat is for if not for cushioning?
A good fall will elicit a pleasant giggle.

Occasionally there will be a teary outburst
provoked by imagination more than pain.
For you can't always laugh when you're falling
even if you know you're in little danger.
I never cried (except to manipulate)
(and now and then when I was at the movies).

Be warned. There are several different versions.
Make sure they have the one from fifty-eight.
Directed by Delbert Mann. I think you'll be
over the moon with this one. Burt Lancaster's
fiery wife, Rita Hayworth, shows up
when he's having an affair with Wendy Hiller.
David Niven gets caught in a sex scandal
whilst trying to befriend Deborah Kerr.

You're a soldier charging into battle
with such ferocity you don't notice your wounds.
Kerr is a virginal hysteric dominated
by her snooty mother, Gladys Cooper.
Wendy Hiller manages to manage
her hotel on a dark and rainy seacoast.

Everything was clean and freshly painted,
butterflies on lawns as smooth as dreams.
Every median was aflush with flowers.
The pregnant moon climbed softly above the trees
and above a department store recently built
over what had been a famed roller coaster.
It was as if I'd seen that moon before
climbing over that department store.

The first year I was here at this same spot
and lunar moment. Little Audrey and I
lay on the rich dark lawn and traded secrets
while being spied on by that radiant zero.
The second year and the third I was here alone.
The first year is the main one I remember.

For sure that's true! We're all made out of sunlight!
It's dark when we close our eyes! What a surprise!
It should be as bright as when we opened them.
Bright as the light we see when we bang our head.
Maybe brighter under certain conditions.
All life's descended from an amoeba suspended
from the line that separates sea from sky,
or maybe earth from fire, brain from brawn.

Just six more lines to go: Adam-Eve
and Satan-God are the Meta Four.
Any old apple can represent the amoeba.
It's a weepy moment whenever we remember
we're all made out of sunlight, billions of beams,
and once we're made of them darkness descends.

My darling fiancée had been working on
a big fat novel for at least five years
and I didn't know a thing about it.
How out of it a serious soul can be!
I didn't read the newspaper the day
her novel was nominated, and later won,
the biggest literary prize in Christendom.
"Hi, sweetie, how are you?" "I'm fine, you?"

But gradually I notice she seems rich
and all her new friends look like Cary Grant.
And last night they say at the Ondaatje soirée
she was doing the cancan on the piano top
wearing a tartan miniskirt (Clan MacPhaidin)
while I was home annotating Ramakrishna.

Sometimes we don't hear that constant beeping
until it stops, then everything is silent.
We weren't listening, then again we were.
A garbage truck is slowly backing up
along the narrow one-way street we live on.
Beepbeepbeep beepbeepbeep beepbeepbeep.
We don't hear it, but in the ensuing silence
it becomes the source of our sudden gloom.

Strange that the beeping didn't bother us
but the silence did. Well, it did and it didn't.
And now that the silence has us listening
the truck will start its beeping once again
and this time we shall listen to every beep.
When the beeps stop silence fools the world.

The Luftwaffe sank four ships in Liverpool harbour.
Auden was writing his "spirit orgulous" poem.
John Lennon was a baby two days old.
Marshal Pétain on the radio was insisting
the French must learn to differentiate
between their friends and their enemies.
He urged collaboration with the Nazis
in rounding up French Jews for deportation.

Born Anastasia Wolochatiuk in Manitoba,
Sister Demetrius that day entered
Alberta's Novitiate of the Sisters Servants.
Over the years she prayed for peace and studied
the sacred scriptures in the Ukrainian tongue.
She died this year at the age of eighty-seven.

When he was a junior all-night proofreader
his senior colleagues were much more laid-back.
Misspell Coca-Cola and there'd be terror
but most words, what the hell, it didn't matter.
This fellow was different, for the smallest error
gave his heart a little jolt of excitement
as if he were a policeman getting a thrill
zapping every word that looked like trouble.

Coincidentally, he was a friendless sort.
He was living a life of solitary squalor
hooked on the thrill you get when you spot an error.
The seniors lacking his speed and accuracy
were slightly nervous about this non-stop jerk.
If this kept up they'd all be out of work.

34

We've often heard it said that cockroaches
have little appreciation for good music.
Don't believe it for a moment, dear friend.
Today I put a slice of bread in the toaster
and when the toaster started to get hot
out from under it came a good-size roach
and sat there frozen in the growing heat.
It probably thought its time had come.

Because we're kind we'd never kill a cockroach
(though we're not above tormenting them to death).
I merely sprinkled holy water on this bug
then blew warm air his way and he didn't budge.
But when I hummed "Danny Boy" in his face
you should have seen his antennae keeping time.

Some faces never change, others are sentenced
every ten years to startling metamorphoses.
If we all looked alike nobody would know us.
We wouldn't have a clue who to screw.
Luckily or unluckily we're distinctively
one of a kind, which is too weird for words.
Though everyone of course likes to do it,
everyone likes to do it differently.

All is glory if minds run that way.
From time to time it gets increasingly
difficult to recall life's rapturous moments.
Sure, deep inside we're all duplicates,
we're all the butt of the self-same rubber stamp,
but some of us are nicer than you others.

It's true Claude seldom talks about himself
but he thinks about himself all the time.
He's always trying to cut down on the amount
of thinking time devoted to himself.
After all, he's not the Dalai Lama
or the newly crowned Pope Benedict XVI.
It'd make more sense to think about those guys
but he'd prefer to think about himself.

The younger are laid low with romantic woe.
The older are obsessed with something stranger.
A very odd obsession: one's own self.
A common vice, but it's not so vulgar,
especially when said self spends most of its time
searching for the source of said obsession.

My nails are sharp and in the crowded train
I accidentally poked a guy in the shoulder
hard enough to make him turn and glare.
I'm sorry, I said, but he continued glaring
then turned away in a huff looking annoyed.
A handsome stalwart samurai soldier
riding to a distant station on a mission.
I thought about it then I tried once more:

Did I poke you in the shoulder? I'm so sorry!
He smiled! And warmly entered into the present
(but in his eye was a note of regret
for having initially taken such offence).
His little girl looked up at him and smiled.
But often a smile will mean "Enough already!"

On a green and flowering hill on the Isle of Chios
I built a hut and covered it with seaweed.
The white carnations and the pale sea breezes
perfume my golden abode all summer long.
And yet I live in sad-hearted solitude —
a Leander without his Hero, drowning in grief —
in the evening gazing at the luminous sky
and the sloping sea, dreaming of my Sappho.

Sappho's my adorable tender nymph
who spreads her soaked tresses to dry in the wind
and leaves her naked body to float on the flowers.
In dreams I've known her love on buttercup beds,
in mossy grottos, on the sandy shore, and I have
tasted pleasures no one could invent.

Now and then we lived in the Frigid Zone,
watching old movies, snowshoeing into town
for a case of Iceberg Vodka and a lottery ticket.
Who gives a hoot if governments are corrupt?
Who cares if the hawks have a stranglehold?
Three-ring circuses aren't our loaf of bread.
Nothing could disturb our *savoir froid*
except for the scarcity of firewood.

We can't offer a magic mirror to breathe on
for breathing on things is not our cup of tea.
We need to read the news but not every day.
What's bubbling now will soon be boiling over.
Only one death to die is our Heart's Sutra
so why not let it happen at the perfect moment?

Dear Librarian: This book is overdue.
No excuses: I just kept forgetting.
In all the forty years I've had this book
other convicts I escorted on weekend passes
were dragged back to the library on time.
But whenever I resolved to return this crook —
The ABC of Reading by Ezra Pound —
some odd spirit would cause me to forget.

Pound's book was published in 1934.
The library acquired it the following January.
I borrowed and read it in 1964
then read it again just the other day.
It's apparently the only copy you had.
Nobody's been able to read it in forty years.

Mr. Sun, you're bright and beaming this morning:
with the energy of a trillion all-night fanatics
in every little wiggle of your red-hot nose.
Wise men say it's bad luck to criticize you.
Sexagenarians stay in on cloudy days.
No one wants to douse the flame that feeds us.
But ... today you look as bright as a beluga
in your rapidly thinning coat of creamy mist.

The spider's webs seem slyer than last year's.
More cunningly weaved and cleverly positioned.
But ... there are no mosquitoes in these webs,
strung between the shadowy cedar branches.
Not that I'm criticizing you, Mr. Sun,
but could it be a bit too hot for mosquitoes?

A fortune cookie came my way that said
You Will Be Awarded Some Great Honour.
I taped it conspicuously to the fridge.
But that sugary augury may have been meant
for you, George Bowering. Why would anyone
give Some Great Honour to some no-good bum
when there stands a specimen such as yourself
lean and eager to receive the loftiest laurels?

We're known for needing no encouragement.
We strive to save our planet from disgrace.
When some poor guy decides to honour himself
the whole world ups and applauds his great debut.
Whenever we think a thought we think worthwhile
we think old George is probably thinking it too.

Claude's life is almost over, he has tattooed
on his back Harvest Organs Freely,
and on his chest, from one droopy tomato
to the other, Get It While You Can.
Just because he can't stand people up close
doesn't mean he can't give them his organs.
Enthusiasm's contagious, so they say ...
but the enthusiasm of others saps him dry.

In his youth he was full of give and take
but now he hates to take and has nothing to give.
His former friends are trying to free the world
from everything that's ruining everything ...
Claude seems to have forgotten how to do that
and/or he no longer cares about the world.

Ralph's dad though Jewish-born became a strictly
conservative Presbyterian minister.
One evening mom and dad were startled when
Ralph threw his dinner at the dining-room window.
When pressed for explanations he said he thought
he saw his English teacher peeking in.
Then they caught Ralph reading dirty books.
He spent two months on the psychiatric ward.

He liked to get dressed up like Barbara Amiel
but in his thirties he became terribly ill.
His girlfriend was snoozing on his bedside chair.
The chair tipped back with a crash. "Lucy! Lucy!
Can't you see I'm trying to die of cancer?"
She laughed, he laughed, he vomited and died.

Call me Diefenbaker. I'm the Prime
Minister of Canada. I'm on the train
heading from Ottawa to Saskatoon
and flipping through the pages of a book
by the poet: George H. Bowering.
Holy smokes! A chapter devoted to me.
I can't understand a word of it
but it's Canadian so it must be good.

Odd coincidence: the lad's from Oliver
and Olive made me promise I'd read his book.
Fields of snow stretch out to the horizon.
And suddenly, leaning against a sagging fence,
a fellow holds up a sign as the train goes by:
George Bowering You Will Never Die.

There's no scaffold, there's nothing holding up
the universe. If we'd heard that said,
by Galileo himself, in Bertolt Brecht's play,
we might have tried to imagine such amazement
and even have succeeded in some way.
Once when Nabokov was free and footloose
he climbed aboard the two-to-two to Toulouse.
The universe is no bigger than the mind.

You're not obtuse, you just need some juice.
So here's a Charlotte Russe for Mr. Moose.
There was a dentist who pulled the wrong tooth.
This wasn't loose and so his goose was cooked.
Now and then Galileo probably said
that all those stars could fit inside your head.

The person writing these lines is very little.
He literally is knee-high to a grasshopper
and marooned as he is in the big city
it's amazing that an ordinary person
hasn't yet crushed him underfoot.
Yes, I am so little it's amazing.
To me a newborn kitten is a monster.
I've never met a soul littler than mine.

By little I don't mean metaphorically
like "disenfranchised" or "dirt-poor in spirit."
Oh no, simply a fellow who's half an inch tall,
who refuses offers to capitalize on his size,
who has learned to leverage a little living
scratching witticisms on windowpanes.

Shakespeare wore a gold ring in his ear.
A friend of his suggested that he do.
My friend Claude, in early photographs,
always appears to be fashion's foe.
Fashion's existence could not be acknowledged
without Claude's life losing its mystery,
and Shakespeare's friend was careful not to throw
the Bard's murmuring mind onto the page.

Claude knew early on he was no good
in a crowd but he liked a surprise.
Shakespeare seldom showed a sign of ambition
or any desire to be in the public eye.
He only desired to sit at his desk and draw
perfect conclusions to inconclusive verses.

No day's complete without a few wrong numbers
and rare is the cat that'll look you in the eye.
I'd rather be a footsoldier than a stinkpot
so I sold my bucket of bolts in '82.
Odd, but straightaway I began to notice
I had more spending money in my pocket.
Heavy metal had been expelled from my heart
and I'd been promoted to a Haydnesque plane.

But motorists tend to despise pedestrians.
Puritans, they hate to see people walk free.
So those on foot will always have to be ready
to accelerate beyond the speed of light ...
and as I typed those dots the telephone rang:
a voice said, "Hello? Hello? Is this Lightspeed?"

In the darkness a wall lizard bumps its snout
against my foot then scampers up my leg.
A kite squawks three times then falls asleep.
A badger waddles through the bushes then
takes a pee on a rock. A dull red star
rises above the dimly outlined peak
then reflects on its glum red dot in silence.
I don't have much to say and so I listen.

A word too many and the poem disappears.
Seagulls bark like a dog protecting its pup.
On the far shore little lights project
their tongues across the surface of the lake.
In the distance a train enters a tunnel.
The songbirds wake up and start to sing.

Like lots of us, the box jellyfish
feeds lazily on small fish and crustaceans.
But its tentacles trail nine or ten feet long.
Swimmers, you'll be sorry if you touch one.
Also notable are its twenty-four eyes.
Unfortunately it doesn't have a brain,
but with such vision what need is there to think?
Or would you prefer a giant brain and no eyes?

Sixteen eyes are merely "pigment pits."
But eight blaze eight times brighter than the human eye.
For its feathers one might wish to be a peacock
but there's something about being a box jellyfish.
I think I'd like to have that blazing vision.
But when would I have any time to think?

He moved into a house of many mansions
on the dark north shore of Lake Ontario.
Elephants, kangaroos and ostriches
trotted along the beach with a watchful air.
Greasy monks in mouldy filling stations
sang the sacred sutras of the world.
Close friends and even ones he'd forgotten
breezed right in and brought him presents too.

He was presented with a ring that with a touch
receives the Top Stories from Other Galaxies.
A bashful boy brought a book about bananas.
The light was swollen and the air was sandy.
Agrimera started begging for forgiveness
and she got it because she loved her name.

Plenty of time left to fill the silence
by making fake entries in blank spaces
and writing poems only mildly sad.
It's January! Look at these empty pages!
I'm sure you'll be able to get through all of them
now that you know there's nothing in them.
Year by year, the yearbook has fewer entries.
If only we knew which page would be our last.

Is it true we can't see anything but
our useless self everywhere we look?
Do I love my devils but hate yours?
Do I prefer myself to all or none?
And if I'm obsessed with hating myself
is it only because I love myself too much?

Dreams are always boring, like last night
I dreamt I was at a same-sex all-Caucasian
wedding party in some dreary church hall
with an Italian band, all male, playing boleros
and a vocalist, a dead-ringer for Little Luigi,
a small man with a slick moustache and a
thin-lipped smile, says he wishes he weren't
Católico, he'd divorce his Metodista wife.

The stupendous visions and ultrasonic nightmares,
the celestial affairs of the heart so super-inspired,
one-of-a-kind splendours never before seen:
these dreams we turn away from and forget,
like a dog turning away from your Fragonard —
no match for another dog's stale breakfast.

Never ride your bicycle with your mouth open;
I swallowed a dragonfly that way one day.
In childhood's exotic dream landscapes
it's better to swallow a dragonfly than a swallow
and the sensation of it dying in my tummy
deep-froze the heart of spontaneity,
like a peek into the universe of footnotes,
one for every tasty treat we've absorbed.

How proud we were we didn't crash our bike.
It's almost as if life itself had meaning.
We vowed we'd never become a mere statistic,
till Aunty June ran off with that mathematician,
that skinny little guy who talked like Bogie
and said we only remember consciousness.

In the middle of the deepest darkest night
a year-old infant awoke in his crib
and everything was silent as a tomb.
Where bare wall would be a picture was hanging,
glowing with otherworldly intensity,
showing a silent sky sprinkled with stars,
fields of perfect white snow to the horizon,
a bright orange tractor dominating the foreground.

Such a picture so perfectly composed!
The child's little mind was illuminated.
Something about this vision was so pluperfect
he knew nothing could be the same again.
It would stay with him all the days of his life
even when everything else would be forgotten.

A steady wind and the waves are coming in
stronger than you'd expect on the shallowest
and the smallest of the five Great Lakes.
The wind is whistling at Featherstone Point.
The waves come in sets of nine-point crescendos,
each crest higher than the one before
until the tenth which will tie for littlest,
a carbon copy of the previous first.

You're a lonely guy sitting on a beached log.
You're eleven or twelve. The wind's still whistling.
And like a Virgin standing on a stone
behind you and above your lowly perch
a woman faces the storm in the thinnest dress
allowing the wind to polish her thighs and breasts.

Claude was sitting in a tiny room in Soho
drinking coffee and trying to stay awake.
The two Michaels (Spinks and Tyson) are fated
to demolish each other at 3:25 a.m.
The night clerk and Claude have a little wager.
Claude took a silly bet there'd be no knockdown
before the end of the sixth round.
But he dozed off and didn't wake till dawn.

He missed it! Tyson knocked out Spinks in the
ninety-first second of round number one.
Claude ran downstairs in his froggy pyjamas
but the night clerk had vanished with the fog.
He was just a temporary, said the day clerk.
Claude was sure his fifty pounds was gone.

He would never fool himself. He truly thought
he perfectly understood practically everything.
Dreams of Being Eaten Alive by David
Rosenberg he was sure he'd never read.
But one night having dined on a Texas T-bone
he dreamt he was hogtied to the undercarriage
of a subway car careening through the dark.
His heart was more than broken, it was throttled.

A few months later, having forgotten the scare,
he had the roast-beef special at the Duke of Kent:
just as our vital essence never stops groaning —
being buried in our body like a corpse —
for hours he heard a child inside him moaning
as its bubbling body turned to Irish stew.

You smelled it here first: solitary flowers,
they have the sweetest scent, even if
one sniff may make you feel a bit peculiar.
Being friendless is better than having what
parents call the wrong kind of friends,
the kind that try to repay your faith in them,
in the winter, when we're absurd, bored,
claustrophobic, sighing for other planets.

When humanity comprises one big heart,
the only friend you'll need will be yourself.
When you honour yourself you also honour
the solitudinous souls of every land.
Let war fade away, let it become
something that simply these days is not done.

A waxing crescent moon shone through the trees.
It was a 1940s Lake Erie-style café.
He was reading the paper, she was not.
She kept glancing at his uneaten hamburger.
She'd eaten hers, now she wanted his.
They understood each other far too well.
She said she generally likes predictable people;
he said he knew she was going to say that.

He saw her fingers creeping towards his burger
so he quickly picked it up and took a bite.
"Don't you put words in his mouth," she said to the
waitress in her snidest tone, "he's eating."
He said, "Is there something wrong with eating?"
"Another burger?" the waitress thought to mumble.

Of being at a baseball game I dreamt.
I moved away from friends and sat alone.
A baseball was hit way up in the stands.
I could have caught it but I didn't want to.
Something that falls from the sky must find
its proper place on the ground. Any idea
that comes to a cardinal on his birthday
should be apprehended cautiously.

This was the final game of the 2006
Pear Tree Series. That ball I've caught before
but I didn't want to take the chance of breaking
a fingernail (though this was merely a dream).
Why bother? And what do my friends care?
That dreamball seemed to smile as it sailed by.

A nervous young poet from Nigeria
looked me in the eye and decided
it'd be safe to tell me about the Abiku,
an evil spirit more powerful than the hungry
ghosts of Tibetan and other world traditions.
The ghosts drink oil from lamps, they're desperate
to be born, and once they manage to be born
most die with no warning and no known cause.

Not even the ritual mutilation of corpses
or the wearing of magic amulets
could stop the Abiku from exerting
a malevolent influence on its environment.
People die under mysterious circumstances.
Her mother and her aunt were both Abikus.

Stan was off to Port Colborne Bible College
to visit Prof. Bowering who'd broken his hip
while refereeing some dogs in his front yard.
When the dogs decided to turn on him
(in a vicious and most terrifying manner)
the Prof. fell on his ass (without spilling
a drop of his tequila) and fractures ensued.
Everything had been going fine till then.

But Stan can't come because he broke his foot
while getting into his Porsche to visit the Prof.
It's almost like a fracture epidemic.
Stan wants to come, Prof. Bowering
wants him to come but Stan's foot is turning
darkly sallow and sore as all get out.

Synonyms are words that like to flirt.
Homonyms are words that are in love.
Antonyms are words that are divorced.
That's what Mrs. McFarland was saying, but Fred
was the only one in all of Grade 2 to get it,
to understand what the teacher was saying.
That's how intelligent Freddy was, my friends.
The teacher would even consult him for advice.

Fred once overheard Mrs. McFarland
bitching about kids to the other teachers at break.
"Freddy's the worst. He's too smart and too cute.
He makes the other kids feel second rate."
Well! That was it for Freddy and his brain.
No one ever noticed either again.

Be perfectly calm as the perfect sea
in the middle of a storm or when it's still,
as the honking of cars in a traffic jam
or the screeching of a streetcar turning home
in the screech-owl middle of the night.
Be calm, honey. When your heart is pounding.
Be extra calm when the bombs are falling
or when soldiers are bashing down your door.

Sometimes we need someone who will thrust
a torch into the darkness of our mind,
illuminating a calmness we never thought
existed though it's been that way forever.
From the centre of our being to the furthest
reaches of nothingness all is calm.

Just when I think I've got all I need
someone comes by and presents me with
something unpredictably unforgettable.
Like that nonagenarian in the coffee shop
who looked at me a while back and stopped
and asked if he could sit down for a moment.
He had a story I might like to hear,
from the time when he was living in Peru.

The Old Man and the Sea was being shot.
Hemingway was visiting the set,
tossing racial slurs around and making
everybody want to strangle him.
No need to describe details. They were ugly.
The village of Cabo Blanco will never forget.

Charles Bukowski apologized to the world
for having spent so much time lifting weights
when he could have read for the same outlay
the complete works of Honoré de Balzac.
It's the tourist psychology or something like it.
You only have two weeks before your spirit
flies back home to the land of the frozen dead.
And you don't want to miss one page of pleasure.

What you've seen or failed to see means nothing.
If there's something we really need to read
we'll certainly read it somehow, let's face it.
Besides, according to the *Afterlife Daily*
death draws us into yet another world
where all of Balzac's on tap any old time.

Nancy knows the stats for all the divisions,
and every morning when she gets the paper,
the furniture in the dugout of her brain
gets shuffled around. What percentage of
her brain cells are occupied with baseball love?
She knows so much she almost knows the winners
before they've won, and details she never forgets.
Take all her tips, but never take her bets.

You or I might have brains enough left over
for something else, say a nervous chat
about how that tornado just missed town.
But she's a leading expert on the Han dynasties.
I've also watched her focussed through several innings
while at the piano playing the Chromatic Fantasy.

Now and then, in a dream, we realize
we're divisible by two however odd.
And if we're still on bad terms it's because
that's our way of distinguishing ourselves.
Perhaps we'll never learn to get along.
What to be: eternal foes or secret
allies in love with the invisible?
Regulars at the Hotel No Fly Zone?

No more denial, now it's confession time.
Whenever you hear those two in the next flat
fighting, your face flashes fiendishly.
You musn't make a sound. You strain to hear.
You fantasize she's telling him that your
poems compared to his are far more interesting.

I wanted to be with you all the time
but there were aspects of my personality
(we were very young) you couldn't stand.
And so I got rid of those nasty aspects.
What could be easier? You were worth it.
We were married at St. James Anglican:
the same church your parents were married in
and my parents as well. Now demolished.

From time to time those aspects would return,
tired of being bound and gagged in the basement.
They demanded the right to come upstairs.
Chipmunks and squirrels witnessed frightful scenes.
The McF's are at it again, the neighbours would cry.
And all of a sudden I knew the jig was up.

You know you're not a nice guy but that's okay.
You probably enjoy meditating
on that lovely good deed you did one time.
If you had an ugly side I'd be surprised.
Did you tell that streetcar driver he had
a low IQ? No no, you say, you didn't.
It just sounded like that. But you can't
remember what it was you actually said.

Just when we think that maybe you're not so bad
there's a bolt from the blue, a streak of nastiness
so ghastly everybody rolls their eyes.
Those lacking your perfection can raise your ire
but you'll toss a dog a bone if he looks sad.
At least if there's someone there to notice.

My old friend Claude is interested in
the Afterlife. He plays his Afterlife tapes.
Off he goes to various planes of existence.
He prays to be sent to where he's needed most.
Once a bomb went off on Bloor Street West
and it was his duty to tell the pizza staff
they were dead and it was time to go.
They thought for sure that they were still alive.

Afterlife tapes don't work for me. I'm too
absorbed in thinking nine times out of ten.
But it ain't right to call it the Afterlife,
for life has neither after nor before.
Why's it always clinging? Why's it opaque?
(In metaphysics it's easy to be a bore.)

You can remember when it was and where
but it just so happens what happened is a blank.
A sudden pang reminds you that once again
something nice had happened, it truly had,
but whatever it was has become a blank.
It was a foggy day on Featherstone Point.
Many things happened on that same day,
and you remember those things very well.

Everyone was making comments about the lovers.
Some of it was ribald but respectful.
And five minutes later, just around the corner
something much more interesting happened —
a woman in a red wool sleeve-length sweater? —
much more worth remembering — but she's gone.

Into the deep dank gorge of Red Hill Creek
rushing around great grey dream-like boulders,
we'd hop from one to another without a slip
up to the foot of heavenly Albion Falls.
Our eyes would blaze like the sun through water.
Even on rainy days. Always on Good Fridays.
Hundreds of little kids with no one to nag them.
It was known as the Good Friday hike.

Then along came a smart developer
who developed an adjacent development.
Did he made some dough out of Native land?
Who can remember and who really cares?
That foolishness was a long time past.
Fabulous motorways are more important.

He dreams that he's an infant in his crib
waking in the silence of the night
for no apparent reason whatsoever.
His diaper's dry and his skin is powdered.
He seems to be afloat and free of care,
so serene he can smile at what comes next:
a flying saucer flying through the wall,
a grey wall and a shining sky-blue saucer.

It's piloted by a laughing little lad
who likes to practise silently passing
through solid walls aided by purest thought.
He's just some spirit looking for a body.
A body that doesn't have a spirit yet.
This ugly brat will be the perfect one.

Now for my nap, or am I having it?
I flip a coin. I call it humanity.
Heads we have intelligence and beauty,
the dignity of poverty and tragedy,
courage in the grip of the unknown.
Tails we have insanity and greed,
bombing of cities and the rape and beheading
of the skinnier nations by fatter ones.

Basically we're a swarming mass of maggots.
Each imago's destined for assassination
or if it's lucky expire like Sheats and Kelley.
But everybody's so kind and eager to help:
they'll dive into frigid water to save a stranger.
The source of all evil? New theory every day.

Imagine living in a world in which
for one year out of every four everyone
had to be continually leapfrogging.
Anybody caught not leapfrogging would be
tossed in special jails surrounded by
fences that wouldn't need to be that high.
You could leapfrog in when it's time for sleep
and leapfrog out when it's time for morning tea.

As long as you continue leapfrogging.
Don't care for the idea? Take him away.
A period of time as important as a leap year
deserves to be known for more than an extra day.
Something that would flavour every day.
Something to keep everyone on their toes.

We're at the funeral — I mean the carnival —
Popeye runs off with the bearded lady's beard.
He wants a grass skirt like Betty Boop's.
Olive's steamed cuz Popeye's in love with Betty.
It's the time of Jim Crow, 1933.
A frightened black man has his head poking
through a hole in the canvas, and Popeye and Bluto
wind up to throw a hardball at you know who.

But Popeye lassoos the other side of the abyss
and drags it closer so he can step across.
And Bluto uproots a giant tree but Popeye
smokes his spinach and punches the tree so hard
when it hits the ground it becomes a casket
and Bluto with folded hands falls into it.

By the time those pension cheques start coming in
you'll no longer give a hoot how you look.
But you were always so terribly adorable
with your angelic curls and innocent blue eyes.
I'd count how often people called you angel,
or darling, and how seldom I was noticed.
The score, at the end, was a hundred to none.
No wonder I was always on the run.

Nowadays, Jack, you're my dearest friend,
but here's a photo of me trying to strangle you.
Reaching into the buggy with evil intent.
No way was I trying to do you harm,
I was just trying to frighten mother into
returning you toot sweet to the Baby Farm.

We fear the disease we bear will never be cured
but will creep along like some nameless someone.
Through our pain we utter odd remarks,
consciously, so when we seem asleep
our cheerful doctors check our charts and say
it'd be better for him were he allowed to die.
Our hearts are getting weary, and that's a thing
we haven't noticed in an attic of leap years.

Our lungs rise and fall. Hard to know why.
We're down on our luck as we often are,
in the sorrow of conversations overheard,
stolen hubcaps, the thing about your mother.
Having to battle with perfection and death
can ruin a perfect day, or what's left of it.

Jesus tells the President where to bomb
and when as well. Who's to say what's wrong?
The Grimm Brothers were really rather nice.
You can't tell an embryo by its number:
the harder you try, the nuttier you become
as everyone seems to have known all along
but nobody told me. I had to figure it out
all by myself. Try not to let it consume you.

They refused to leave their homes and so
we had no choice but to bomb and shell.
They'd be proud if they understood
(and if we did I'm sure we would be too).
I suppose it's just because Jesus insisted.
At least that's what the President declared.

You take time off to conceal cancellations
and everything is going the way you want.
You set aside a weekend for silent thought
and by Monday you think you might be dead.
You feel like calling your dead friends to come over.
From now on you can be a floating cloud.
Never again will you worry about your shadow.
Even your toes seem to be ungrounded.

But things are never as good as we pretend.
Things were going swimmingly until
I slipped and fell on your mirror image
and decided to cancel all concealments.
That which is hot will usually still be warm
long after that which is warm has become blah.

We say to poets, "I know you're not a socialist."
They say, "Of course we are." But when we ask
if they count syllables they deny it.
Some deny it but you can tell they count.
Some deny it but say they play by ear.
Matters naught to us you count no syllables.
Nor does it matter you're not a socialist.
We like your haikus about cats and moths.

North America is beginning to look as if it
might become the next South America.
Europe could be transposed to Peru.
But still I'd worry about your pets and insects,
as Tiryns still bemoans its ancient citadel,
poorly restored seven thousand years ago.

London's warm, humid, overcast and misty.
People are visiting from around the world.
Where are you from? "Nigeria. Just got in."
An Aussie pornographer on AM radio
praises the movie *Misty Beethoven*
and says a third of his customers are female.
Japan has the heaviest Mafia involvement.
I wander into St. Dunstan's in Fleet Street.

A statue of the Virgin Queen's been excavated
and installed above the door of the sacristy.
In a kitchen accident the violinist
severed a nerve in her finger. This is her first
appearance in a year and she's nervous.
But she plays powerfully to proper applause.

Virginia the Romanian electronics engineer
called her pup for unknown reasons Beauty.
She was coming down with Beauty under her arm.
At the ground floor Beauty and Virginia got out.
I was in the lobby, I saw them get out.
Virginia put Beauty down and we chatted
about how Beauty was the best thing in her life.
We looked around and Beauty disappeared!

Virginia was having a fit and so was I.
We tried to figure out what could have caused
Beauty to vanish like that, leaving us trembling,
paralyzed with panic and indecision.
We finally found her on the fourteenth floor
waiting for the elevator to open.

It's an entire high-school football team
in full uniform, with cleats, helmets, pads,
marching single file along Yonge Street,
then disappearing down the Eglinton Station.
Like something out of Fellini. Across the street
I had a perfect view, but everyone else
was busy shopping and didn't give a hoot
if the players had to pay their own fares.

I'd been waiting for my friend Solecki.
He'd quarterbacked his high-school football team
the year they won the provincial championship.
His school in Niagara Falls wore red and white.
My school in Hamilton wore red and white.
And that Fellini team was wearing red and white.

There was too much sugar in the omelette
on the train from Toronto to Montreal.
He read *Caesar of the Wilderness* all the way.
And as he read he kept removing his
Anti-Free Trade button, admiring it
then putting it back on. This was the first
time he'd ever worn a political button
of either kind. It felt uncomfortable.

There's a certain pressure of his mind
that clouds his wispy consciousness and keeps
his spirit slumbering: a vast unleashed
interwoven wilderness of thought
you'd have to be a genius to decode.
Some genius who would do it just for fun.

This morning when I opened up my window
through heartfelt leaves all sparkling with dew
soft pinky rays of light came streaking in.
High in the clouds behind the distant hills
floated a perfect image of Jesus Christ
and (as I watched) Christ's sad face dissolved
into the face of a radiant Dick Cheney
beaming down his blessings from above.

This was a big Dick Cheney, for it stretched
silently from horizon to the zenith.
In each celestial arm it bore a baby
wrapped in swaddling clothes, a Baby Rice,
and, pure pleasure, a Baby Bush, coo-cooing.
Had I visioned that which is to come?

Congatulations, Claude, upon getting your
licence to drive renewed at the age of ninety.
I know you studied night and day for the test.
Too bad three questions missing from the book
gave you some trouble so you left them blank
and at the end you decided to ESP them.
You must have got them right because you passed.
I'm sure they weren't questions of life and death.

It's not easy for nouns to discard their adjectives
but it'd blow your mind how soon you'd learn to cope.
Giving up something so important presages
a passage into a transfer of energies
from the squeal out there to the squall within.
You'll keep driving long as you keep passing.

Life is sad and kind of sticky too.
Twenty years ago, bpNichol
was the most perfect poet of his age.
In his multi-volume *Martyrology*
he invented bright new hubcaps of verse
filled with the finest letters of the alphabet.
But he suffered years of undiagnosed agony
without complaint then died at forty-four.

Even the most unlikely people grieved
and petitioned the city to commemorate his name
on the ragtag road that ran by Coach House Press —
now known as bpNichol Lane. And then last night
while giving a public reading from my book *Glue*
I mentioned bpNichol and nobody knew.

When I first crossed the Peace Bridge into Buffalo
a cricket match was playing on the green.
I caught a golden carp in a contest
in a lake in the middle of Delaware Park.
It would have won for sure but a tough
kid came by insisting I'd stolen his fish.
He was such a bully I said he could have it.
He's probably a Senator by now.

Remember Miles Davis at the Town Casino?
Count Basie at Kleinhan's Music Hall?
Joe Williams at the bar of the Blue Moon?
The whole country now has gone bananas.
Best to avoid eye contact with the natives
and don't pay attention to the traffic lights.

As soon as the dragon (it's a constant battle)
is knocked out it will come alive again.
It's like the cool moon as you're dozing off
suddenly appearing outside your toolbox.
Or like that hot shot blazing in the sky
when you've been freezing all night in the ditch.
It's like eleven o'clock in the morning
of November the eleventh, 1918.

We use our breath and our solar plexus
to download mental pressure moment by moment.
It seems to be getting easier all the time
but there's no compelling evidence of that.
It's like an absence of pain, an inability
to remember what the screaming was all about.

If life is an engagement with history
then even a butterfly can make a difference.
But think of the differences that could be made
by the commander in chief of a superpower
alone in his office fluttering his powdery wings.
He decides to flatten a few more fatherlands.
And every dominion destroyed, lest we forget,
makes the superpower a little safer.

That's the theory as I understand it.
Slaughtering civilians can't really be much fun.
At the courthouse, enjoying the general grief,
you'll know for sure that you have made a difference.
And if you spend ten years in Fort Maple Leaf
you'll be studying up on the history you've changed.

You went out to play without permission.
You sat naked on the photographer's pony.
It was time for you to stop sucking your thumb.
The girls next door could recite the alphabet.
They never wanted you to be around.
You thought you'd landed on the wrong planet.
You knew that life on Earth would not be pleasant.
It was time for you to try to stop your crying.

You went home to play with your hockey stick.
See how high up the stairs you could fire the puck.
Aunty June told you twice to stop that racket.
You ran down the alley with Aunty June chasing.
I'll get him for you, June, said Barry Bottomley.
Leave him alone, said June. I'll get him myself.

What kind of a life is this? I'm twenty-eight
and have no house, no inheritance, no dog.
I'm walking north out of snowbound Berlin
with a box of books and no curiosity.
I seem to have forgotten all I know.
You must see for the sake of a single book
that if it's old it's probably pretty good.
Yes, it must be pretty good to be old.

They say that now my eyesight has returned
it's time I started to try some serious work.
But to be good, you'd have to be pretty old.
You've seen many cities and many people.
You've always paid attention to the new.
So you know anything good must be old.

After Rilke

Some strange god, wishing us great felicity,
fills our sleeping minds with strange montages,
lengthy extravaganzas so complex
awake we find them more or less opaque.
Why show me this, dear spirit? Or why that?
Why in this Cuban night did you show me
two cars colliding and four occupants
tossed under the wheels of a speeding bus?

Such agony! Heads crushed, limbs torn off.
In vivid technicolour with many replays
and different angles. I can only think
some spirit wishes me to be aware
that we must be awake to possibilities
we may or may not be able to anticipate.

Like anything that lacks firm boundaries
poetry's not easy to talk a — FLASH!
The President has won the war on terror!
Let me be the first to congratulate him.
Who to kill now we've killed the killers?
Shall we round up all the union leaders
and ask them to line up at Niagara Falls
like the Carmelites queuing up for the guillotine?

Some gaze at stars, others contemplate clouds,
but there's always someone to resent your views.
Who wouldn't desire to draft a lovely sonnet
about fluffy clouds floating in a fluffy sky?
Who wouldn't prefer to be precise and rational,
cooler on top than bottom, just like clouds.

If you're like me your restlessness will fade.
Mine's fading now, my days and nights sail by
so serenely I seldom open my toolbox.
Doing nothing but reading *American Splendor*,
writing poems and going for silent walks
among the silent people and silent traffic.
Sometimes silence occurs gradually;
sometimes it occurs when least expected.

Given our respectable demographics,
the trajectory of our lives has been explosive.
Nothing smooth, everything hairy and scary,
transformations and surprise separations.
Soon our psychoses will start to give us up.
Chance objects, when observed, will sicken us.

We kids tried hard to pay attention to
what the kids were doing in the U.S.A.
(we were only fifty miles from the border)
and we discovered that their kids approved
of watching ballgames through a hole in the fence.
So we hiked down to the ball park and searched
for a hole in the fence, but this wall was well made
and nowhere could we find a decent view.

Percy went home because he had no money
but I had just enough to watch the game
in the wide-open arms of the happy stands.
Percy claims to have dreamt of being Pyramus
standing all night at the chink in the wall
waiting for Thisby to climb down from the moon.

All my life I've listened to old men bragging:
"Not me, I have no regrets, none at all ...
and you, my masochistic little friend,
if you were smart you'd get rid of yours."
But what about the time you shot the sheriff?
Don't you wish you'd left your gun at home?
And what about the time you robbed that bank?
And what about the time you spent in jail?

"As for the sheriff it was just a flesh wound
and to show his friends he has a scary scar
for which he'll have no end of sympathy
even if they'll be laughing behind his back."
That's nice, but taking pride in my regrets
every day I try to accumulate more.

We're all aware of every little anxiety:
nuclear submarines threatening the coasts,
guided missiles threatening the cities.
But I only get neurotic about you.
You've only been gone a day and I've collapsed.
People are stepping over me on the street.
We're so lucky to have been born in time
to witness a world going down the drain.

So come back soon — how can I enjoy
the collapse of civilization without my honey?
Oh I could but it wouldn't be much fun
not knowing where you are et cetera.
On this almost certain end of the world
who could have someone nicer to chitchat with?

A farmer and his wife had a son
born when they were getting on in years.
One day when the farmer was planting rice
a friend came running up and said the boy
had taken ill and was close to dying.
When the father got home his son was dead.
His wife wept buckets, but he wept not at all.
"Don't you have even one tear to shed?"

The night before he'd dreamt he was a king.
He was the father of seven noble princes,
beautiful, virtuous, kind and studious:
should he weep for the seven or the one?
For some, said Ramakrishna who told this story,
being awake is no more real than dreaming.

Jack Kerouac and his comrade Jack O'Lantern —
would hang out at a bar called Misty Moon
all day every day so I've been told.
When we're not in love, both Jacks mourned,
we lack an audience for our poetry.
Someone drew a picture on the wall.
The boss was annoyed and ejected Jack K.
but for some reason allowed Jack O. to stay.

It was almost like a story from the Bible:
the boy who ran away and then came back.
Decades later the bartender is programmed
to discuss Kerouac, but not O'Lantern.
Talking about O'Lantern confuses the tourists.
Come on, you whispered. Let's get out of here.

For ever so long ago you always were
an oddball, with nasty jokes that only you
could dream up, in fact they were so painful
it's a wonder no one punched you in the nose.
Such strange behaviour, it's as if you chose
these jokes to torture your friends over and over.
We torture everybody we can't deal with.
As if they wouldn't have given us the world.

Don't ever forget how fond we were of you,
while making sure we gave you plenty of room.
And no doubt you had your moments when
you lavished more generosity on yourself
than you ever did on others for all I know.
And I'm pretty sure I'd know if anyone did.

Always honest with himself, that's you.
Many times you've been far too understanding.
Too quick to apologize for the faults of others
and always hoping they will turn a new leaf.
You see the obscurities but not that clearly,
not in any way that would annoy anyone
or inspire them to change their name and address.
It'd be nice to have a charming boat to sail.

If there's charity in you it's not in your heart
or any other organ you could name.
No one, not even the author of these lines,
ever referred to you as subtle or wise.
You think peace is just around the corner
while I've turned into a full-blown mourner.

In Grade 1, Bobby K. Zombory made
plasticine cars run over plasticine people.
At the end of the day the cars would be intact
but he'd be collecting the severed limbs.
Imaginary folks would gather and commiserate
with the motorist as if he'd been the victim
and the cops would tell the motorist not to worry:
any case like this it's the pedestrian's fault.

Like most kids in our town and in our day
Bobby K. dropped out first chance he got.
It was sensational to be liberated and to thumb
rides to visit his sweetheart down by the river.
One day as he stood with his thumb stuck out
a highway patrol car struck and killed him dead.

Did you see my picture in the paper
when I won the lottery? I wondered …
if you'd maybe heard that I had won it?
Every picture taken I was thinking
about you, you could tell by my bright eyes
searching for you inside every flashbulb.
I'm being foolish but I wish I knew
where you are or whatever happened to you.

Even after all these years I'll ponder
the map of my indifference, and envision
the overwhelming non-existence of yours.
That afternoon, you having lost the rent money …
who knows what you were thinking? I don't know.
I'd love to know but it's far too late for that.

In one of the major works of Thomas Mann,
your Rosafarbenestein's described so prettily,
Family Giselle and Erhard Wolf of Bavaria.
Hope you never tire of hearing this song.
I wished to prove Mann's descriptive accuracy.
I found a photograph and I succumbed.
Life would be sweet in such a sweetheart castle.
Reading books and dreaming. Any chance?

Mother Goose bumps covered me all over
as I waited prayerfully for their reply:
"Dear sir, we don't live in Rosafarbenestein.
Our hotel, however, is in the same village.
And you are right, here is a small paradise.
Maybe see you someday ... Kind regards."

The earth's a grapefruit rotting in the sun.
The maggots that infest it have been evolving
and have been testing tiny nuclear bombs
not strong enough to cause serious damage.
But a holy mountain cave-dweller nearby
predicts the imminent transfiguration
of the human race and its unholy descant.
If maggots can get along how come we can't?

The people who believe in so-and-so's theory
won't get mad when their neighbours disagree.
But why should China hit the bloody roof
because Tibet wants to remain aloof?
Perhaps the human race is not the greatest.
Perhaps the maggots will exterminate us.

When we were dimwitted kids at school
we had to learn a lot of poetry.
Shakespeare was pretty good except he was
awfully hard to understand at times.
Yeats and Keats sometimes penned a good line
but most of what they wrote seemed fraudulent.
And why did we have to memorize Shelley
who was always dramatizing the obvious?

The teachers used to say it was bad and sad
that Canada didn't have any poets.
And so we vowed that we would become one.
Seemed like a noble thing to do.
And if Canada needed us we'd be there
to forge a nation with our perfect lines.

If we must die let's die peacefully
stepping out of one shoe into another —
let the other be a better fit.
Round the clock the world blows itself up —
some say paradise can be found on earth,
the best dying and the worst feeling fine.
Though fake paradise would seem better than nothing
nothing probably is best of all.

If the world must die let it die peacefully
and not with nuclear bombs and machete raids.
If we can't live with style let's die with style.
Let all the countries of the world erect shrines
to protect and explain our cultural differences.
Someone might stop off in time to come.

As far as my friend Claude says he's concerned
the "war between good and evil" is more truly
a war between "evil and evil." We'd been watching
the latest news and drinking Canadian Club.
How's about a war between good and good?
He purses his lips as he does when he's thinking.
"That might work," he says. "Can you think of one?"
I knew I couldn't but I pretended I could.

If I could would you like to enlist?
"Are you kidding? I'm a nonagenarian."
But a war between good and good couldn't be bad.
Couldn't you love a planet where the only war
was the war between good and good? "Maybe, but
I'd want to know who gets to define 'good.'"

Cuba's famous for its independence.
New Zealand for its blend of Maori and Scot.
Australia for its sheep and kangaroos.
Canada for its wanton disregard.
Ireland has a wicked sense of humour.
Scotland's crisscrossed with Pictish walls
while Wales is noted for the deepest wells
and England's famed for its bells and balls.

But what can we say about the U.S.A.?
Satchmo! Marilyn Monroe! Allen Ginsberg!
Everything is totally terrific!
You should read up on their democratic system.
In the big things, as we know, they have it right,
and also too they've got the little things right.

No proud and proper spider would ever spin
a web between two shells of an empty peanut.
But this one did, and boy was I surprised.
Of all the nooks and crannies in the house,
why should these two half shells attract a spider?
Maybe because the web's pattern's imprinted
on the shell of every peanut in the world,
even the highly addictive Sudanese peanut.

And so that little spider must have thought
those shells had a friendly look about them.
He settled down between their fraternal arms.
But later you could see the web was stretched
like a silent night over a baseboard hole
out of which the occasional roach might stray.

Glad you decided to spend a week at Green Lake.
Wish I could join you, we could have a lark,
swimming rivers, wandering in the hills,
but always on the lookout for grizzly bears.
Meanwhile, I'm reading a novel full of green,
the characters have green-gold eyes and hair,
and now and then a crème de menthe or two.
Green parrots make green patterns in the air.

Defence mechanisms have been tinted green.
The sky is sea-green, and the sea is sky-green.
It's almost as if we're in the land of the green
and no one's blue anymore and no one's yellow.
Everybody's turning green with envy,
as am I, knowing you're up at Green Lake.

No one knows beans about the major crimes.
Only officials believe the official story.
On the streetcar everyone's eating hotdogs.
We've entered a world without stereotypes.
My dreams tell me the President doesn't know
anything but the funny stories he's told.
I walk into Camp David, he slaps my back.
I must confess to feeling warm and fuzzy.

Would I have dreamt that if he'd known anything?
He even spoke a fluently civil English
and so did I. (Oh, if we could write
as well as we could speak we'd never speak.)
Did you know so-and-so gassed his own people?
Something's not quite right but what the hell.

The most well-known of Shakespeare's sonnets by far
are the ones a woodchuck could relate to.
Everyone understands envy, even those
fortunate enough to think they've outgrown it.
And everyone understands the sorrow that
deepens and widens with each passing year.
And discontent's a perennial favourite. Wow!
His sonnets seem to be all about me!

And so we sad-eyed votaries thrill to these poems
at the expense of the happier, more difficult:
the "general of hot desire," and poems about
"nymphs that vowed chaste life to keep" who come
tripping by to view the "little Love-god"
sleeping beside his "heart-inflaming brand."

Except for the morning following a dream
he seldom thinks about her anymore.
She'd now be sixty but he hasn't seen her
except in dreams since she was forty-two.
He senses she's as lovely as she was.
In some dreams she'll look then turn away.
In other dreams she'll be more forthcoming
but other people will start distracting her.

In those dreams she's always forty-two.
Of the man he's become would she approve?
Like most of us, he's lost his sense of humour.
He has money but he keeps losing it.
His friends drag him out to cultural events
but most of the time he hangs out at home.

The children saw their father slaughter the pig.
The older said to the younger, "You be the piggy
and I'll pretend I'm the butcher. It'll be fun."
He took the shiniest sharpest knife he could find
and slit the throat of his cute little brother.
The mother was upstairs bathing the baby
and when she heard the cries she ran downstairs.
Nothing like this had ever happened before.

She was so upset she took the knife
and killed the older boy. Then dashed upstairs
only to find the baby had drowned in the tub.
Neighbours arrived but mother refused all comfort.
She saw her husband coming from the fields,
so she hanged herself ... and so did he.

After Jack Zipes

While reading chapter 13 of *Aimez-vous Brahms?*
(a 1959 ménage à trois, madame)
I thought it'd be fun to put on some
Brahms Piano Sonatas as played by Perahia.
Though like others I have never excelled
at listening and reading at the same time,
a little Brahms while reading Françoise Sagan
will crystallize every word in the book.

But listen up, readers. Here's something to ponder.
At the end of chapter 14 I flicked on the telly
to see what old movie was being shown
on Silver Screen Classics on Channel 320.
It just happened to be *Aimez-vous Brahms?*
with I. Bergman, Y. Montand and T. Perkins.

At least a thousand times I've sunk that basket
but this time I missed it and we lost
the Hamilton East high-school championship
and it's all my fault. How will my parents
handle this at church on Sunday morning?
My kid brother won't know where to hide.
But Emerald Downdaughter won't mind.
She'll likely find it increases my allure.

Emerald was a cute tough-talking high schooler
and I was her secret boyfriend for a while.
Once I said, "Look! A shooting star!"
then asked how come she didn't turn and look.
She said it would be gone before one could.
Ruby Divine, she also liked to be called.

Those wrens and songbirds coming up from Cuba,
they're singing but they're not so very merry.
How were they to know Toronto would be
icebound still on the eleventh of March?
We were friendly but they were very wary.
It seemed we didn't seem all that trustworthy.
Maybe they thought we wanted to pop them in
the oven for a feast of songbird pie.

Were they fingering us folk for the freeze?
Our instincts tell us birds are fully capable
of thinking. Unless you want to think the singing
of the birds of the forest thoughtless.
Not that this is the forest. It's still Toronto.
A Holy Hogtown frozen, silent, brooding.

The chestnuts are in blossom for so long
you don't really miss them when they've gone.
Unlike the cherry blossoms that cover the path
so soon it hurts your heart to see them go.
I'm writing about flowers to encourage them
to remember spring is coming in two days.
Toronto's torrents of spring can be tender.
Who cares if there's a foot of snow out there?

As for sentient beings, we're aware
that spring is about to tune up its string
and play a little song we'd almost forgotten.
But especially for the poor and hibernating
with bones so weak they can't get out of bed —
as the blossoms fade and fall we'll die too.

The place I most remember mud was Fruitland —
and Winona, long ago in early spring,
hiking along the base of the Niagara escarpment.
And I was having that quicksand sensation.
Oh-oh, am I into this too deep?
And just when I could hardly summon the strength
to lift a sucking leg for another step
I had to go to the toilet, number two.

Tanizaki, in his famous novel,
far more famous than the eponymous movie,
describes swarms of fireflies in the night,
and little streams that ran through the paddies.
It would all be mud in a week or so.
The novel was *The Makioka Sisters*.

I visited my Granma in the nursing home.
She looked at me blindly and deafly
and said, When you're as old as I am
in dreams you'll meet people you haven't seen
in fifty years so plain you can touch their nose.
She'd been dreaming of her first husband again.
She knew how to grieve but she also had
both senses of humour: subtle and slapstick.

She loved her furs and her jewellery
and would carry a silver flask in her purse.
Some found her simple but she was brilliant
in her own way and on that day she said:
There's nothing I want to see anymore
and there's nothing anymore I want to hear.

A Cupid is snoozing on a cloud, his head
resting on his arm which rests on his pillow.
An airplane flies directly through his brain
and out his backside without him even knowing.
I was taking a moment to check out the sky.
There were many other clouds that Cupid
could have napped on, but he chose this one,
snoozing by my window, as if he knew.

He and the cloud were moving slow and steady.
Stately too would also be a word.
But what could we say about the plane?
The pilot seemed very, very experienced.
The plane was moving very fast and straight.
Passing through Cupids would never slow him down.

Professor Norris, the poet of personalism,
when spring breaks, hops on planes and flies
over sweet but salty seas to happy islands.
Yet he extrapolates on the unappreciated.
He advocates each J. K. Rowling adopt
some worthy poetic beacon of poverty,
cultivate him or her with annual stipends.
An honourable thought for a personalist.

Now the professor wants to chuck his job.
To become a penniless poet is his desire.
Talk me into it or out of it, he implores.
A wave crashes against a rugged cliff.
Norris needs to listen to those angelic
voices within, not satanic ones like mine.

When my mother died I saw her standing
alone at midnight at some railway station,
standing tall and very businesslike.
Suddenly our arms were around each other
in an eerie darkness bright as noon.
We were the only people on the platform
in a force field far too deep for sparks.
She broke from me and vanished in the train.

She was different than she'd been in life.
She was everything I ever wanted.
I was certain I would never see her again.
She had to go to some unknown world.
The train pulled out silently and empty.
I was the only person left on the planet.

January 2004 – June 2008

ACKNOWLEDGMENTS

To Stuart Ross for his kindness, friendship, energy, and over-the-wall enthusiasm.

To Denis De Klerck for the amazing cover illustration and design, and for catching that nasty typo in Sonnet 121.

To Gordon Carruth of Ottawa, my grade 13 French teacher, for addressing me as Monsieur le Poète in front of the class.

To my dear friend (and former spouse) Joan Tressel, our daughter Jennifer C. McFadden, my brother Jack and my father William.

To Christina Prozes and the ever-expanding Estonian connection, including Annaliisa Luik, Viive Tork and Rob Hiis.

To Zasep Tulku Rinpoche and the Tibetan connection.

To everyone who still remembers the late great Greg Curnoe.

To Norma Morrell, who taught me the joy of reading when I was three years old, and also taught me to recite the alphabet frontwards, backwards and sideways.

And a special tip of the hat to the late but unforgettable Alison J. Bennett (1964-2000).

Some of these sonnets appeared previously in *This Magazine* and *Syd & Shirley*.

Photo: Lorianna De Giorgio

David W. McFadden lives and works in Toronto and is the author of numerous books of poetry, fiction and non-fiction. He has been nominated for the Governor General's Award twice (*The Art of Darkness* in 1984 and *Gypsy Guitar* in 1988). He was short-listed for the 2008 Griffin Poetry Prize for his book *Why Are You So Sad? Selected Poems of David W. McFadden* (Insomniac Press, 2007).